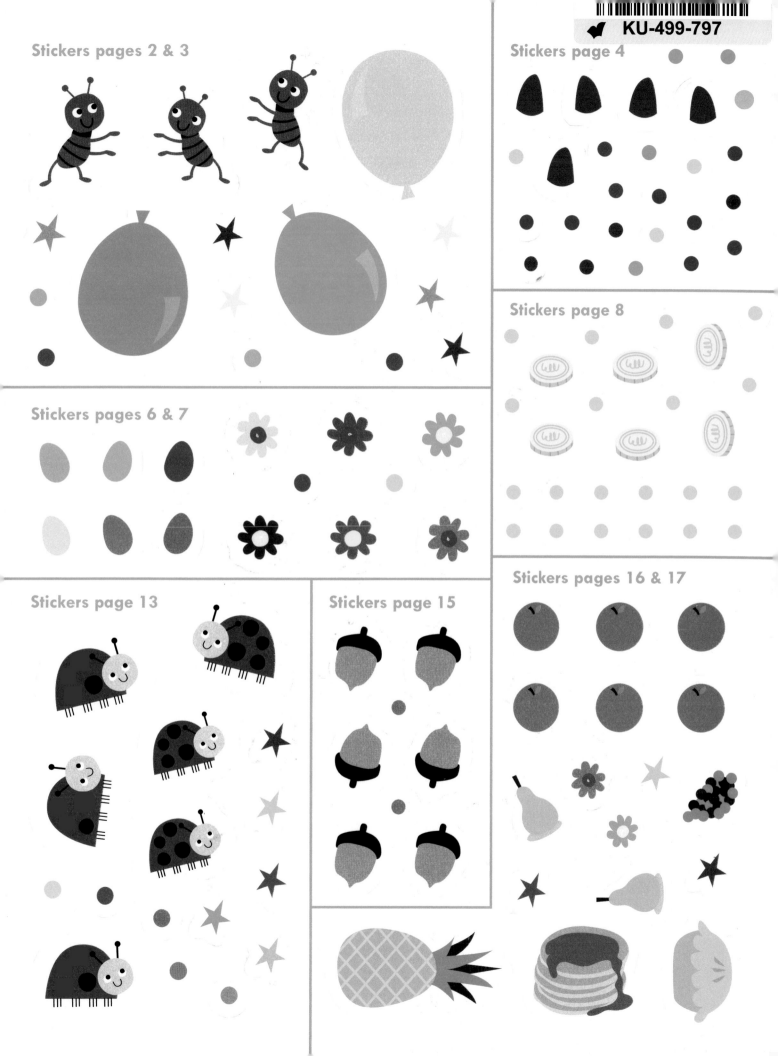

Stickers pages 2 & 3

Stickers page 4

KU-499-797

Stickers page 8

Stickers pages 6 & 7

Stickers page 13

Stickers page 15

Stickers pages 16 & 17

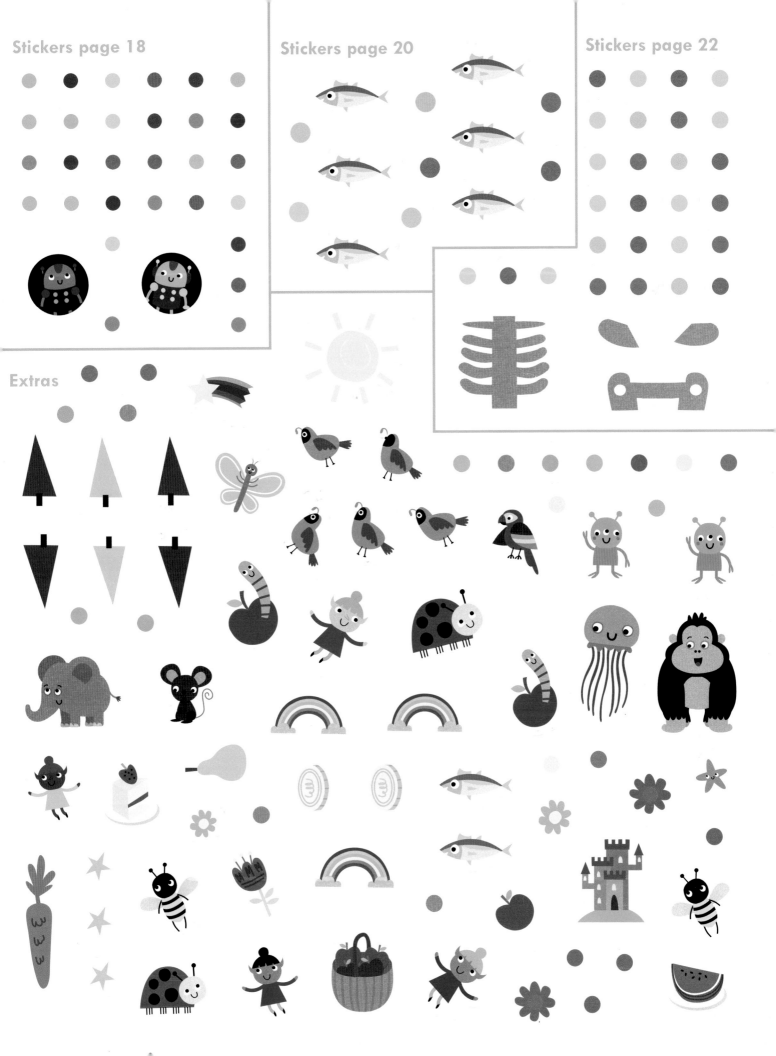

Stickers page 18

Stickers page 20

Stickers page 22

Extras

Bb

Bear wants big balloons. Use your stickers to finish the picture.

Can you find five buzzing bees?

Trace the word.

bee

Cc

Use your stickers to decorate my cake.

How many candles can you count?

Trace the word.

cat

4

Dd

Colour in the spotty dinosaur

I'm a Diplodocus!

Can you find five dragonflies?

Trace the word.

dino

5

E e

Can you find the elephant that matches this picture?

Sticker more eggs in the nest.

Trace the word.

egg

Ff

Sticker pretty flowers.

Trace the word.

fun

Colour the flamingoes in pink.

Can you find five fairies?

7

Gg

Growl!

Use your stickers to give the gorilla lots of gold.

Trace the word.

gold

8

Hh

Hooray!

Colour in the horses' hats.

Trace the word.

hat

9

Ii

Ladybird Butterfly Worm Bee Dragonfly

Trace the word.

island

10

Kk

Follow the lines to see which
kite belongs to the king.

Trace the word.

king

Ll

Count my spots!

Sticker lots of ladybirds on the leaves.

Trace the word.

leaf

13

Mm

Help the little mouse through
the maze to his mum.

FINISH

START

Trace the word.

mouse

Pp

Sticker food on the plates for the panda's picnic.

Trace the word.

pie

17

Qq

Trace the word.

queen

Decorate the queen's quilt with stickers.

Rr

Sticker robots in the rocket.

Trace the word.

red

What colour is the rocket?

S s

Colour in the stripy snakes.

Hisssssssssss

Trace the word.

sun

T t

Draw over the dotted lines to finish the turtle.

Trace the word.

tide

20

Sticker more tuna fish.

Uu

Draw an umbrella over the unicorn

Trace the word.

under

Vv

Can you find the van that matches this picture?

Trace the word.

van

21

Ww

Sticker spots on the whale.

Trace the word.

wet

Xx

Trace the word.

box

Sticker the missing bones to finish the X-ray.

22

Yy

Trace the lines to finish the yo-yo, then colour it yellow.

Trace the word.

yellow

Zz

Give the zebra zigzag stripes.

Trace the word.

zoo

23

A B C D E

F G H I J K

L M N O P

Q R S T U

V W X Y Z